The potential for disaster on D-Day was huge. 156,000 troops with supporting armour were to be landed by sea and air in a surprise attack on the Normandy coast to begin the liberation of continental Europe.

Five beaches, extending over 100km (60 miles), were designated by Allied planners, but the nature of the Normandy coastline meant that the two American beaches, Utah and Omaha, would in the initial assault be isolated both from each other and the Anglo-Canadian sector to the east. While the D-Day objective was to establish a continuous bridgehead up to 10km (6 miles) deep enveloping the main Caen-Cherbourg highway, the plan at Omaha, much the most strongly defended of the D-Day beaches, was far removed from the reality of events.

Here some 60,000 men and 7,700 vehicles, two-thirds of the American effort, were to be concentrated on breaching the German defences. Within seconds of the ramps going down, troops were being slaughtered on the beach by an invisible enemy, while more men, vehicles and a flood tide were pouring in behind and around them. At 0830 hours the landings were suspended and General Bradley even considered diverting the remaining shipboard troops onto Sword. He later wrote: 'I gained the impression that our forces had suffered an irreversible catastrophe.'

By nightfall victory was assured, but at Omaha over 1,000 men had been killed, 3,000 wounded and three-quarters of the equipment lost. At Omaha beach the whole future of the war and of civilization itself had trembled in the balance. What had gone wrong? Why did they have to land here and why were over half the casualties of D-Day sustained here? How did the Americans carry the day in what has been called 'one of the great feats of arms in US history'?

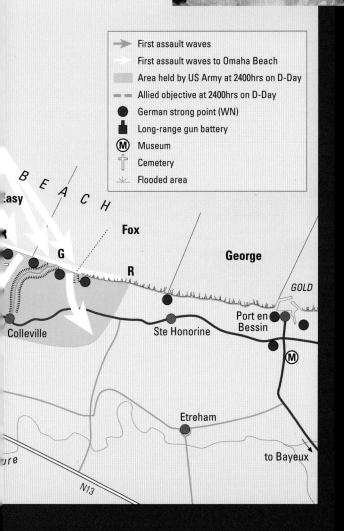

	1 mile
	1 km

→ First assault waves
→ First assault waves to Omaha Beach
█ Area held by US Army at 2400hrs on D-Day
▬ Allied objective at 2400hrs on D-Day
● German strong point (WN)
■ Long-range gun battery
Ⓜ Museum
✝ Cemetery
↯ Flooded area

BEACH

Easy

Fox

G

George

R

GOLD

Colleville

Ste Honorine

Port en Bessin

Etreham

to Bayeux

N13

A TERRIBLE PROSPECT

'The [Wehrmacht was] the most professionally skillful army of all time.'
GENERAL EISENHOWER

Omaha beach was the perfect defensive position: crescent-shaped, 7,000 metres (7,650 yards) long, flanked by sheer cliffs to east and west, and backed by steep 40–50 metre (44–55 yard) bluffs. At high tide there was no beach, at low tide 400 metres (440 yards) of sand flats.

The eastern part of the beach also featured a steeply sloping shingle bank which, with the burning high grass between it and the bluffs, and the irregular folds in the bluffs themselves, provided limited cover for the troops that could reach them.

Five gullies, or draws, led off the beach up through the bluffs. Inland lay the three villages of Vierville, Saint-Laurent and Colleville, connected by a road parallel with the coast. Beyond that lay the claustrophobic hedgerow country known as the 'bocage'.

The bulk of Hitler's army was stationed far away from here. For Hitler, the war was above all a land war against Russia. The troops normally stationed in Normandy reflected this: a motley collection of 'striplings and grey-beards'; officers recuperating from wounds and frostbite; nationals recruited from occupied Eastern Europe and the Russias. The 'static' divisions were often dependent on horse transport, and were desperately short of medical supplies and ammunition. Moreover, they were protected by barely 100 Luftwaffe aircraft.

Despite these poor circumstances, most soldiers were obedient, dedicated and trained to perform beyond the call of duty. Apart from artillery and transport, their equipment outclassed that of the Allies. Cool in combat, they were often fanatically devoted to the Fuhrer. Furthermore, after four years of occupation, they knew the intricacies of the landscape. Most dangerous and determined of all were the new young conscripts, and the SS.

In January, 1944 Rommel was placed in charge of the Northern coastal defences. The Field Marshal understood that the first 24 hours of the forthcoming battle would decide the

ABOVE: Rommel reinforced coastal defences, but his advice was overruled when it came to the strategic use of resources.

BELOW LEFT: Omaha's curve shows the potentially murderous effect of enfilading (end to end) fire.

outcome of the whole war. He fully expected landings in Normandy, but was denied troop reserves to back this hunch. His response was to upgrade beach defences with all speed.

Omaha received much of his attention, for he understood that, despite its defensive advantages, it was an obvious place for an amphibious landing. By defending Omaha, Rommel knew he would be protecting 50km (30 miles) of coast.

Heavy gun batteries were built on the clifftops at Longues and the Pointe du Hoc to the east and west of the beach. The guns, firing nine rounds a minute, could hit ships and beaches up to 20km (12 miles) away.

Within the Omaha beach area, concrete fortifications and defences multiplied. Above all it was vital to defend the five draws, the only exits from the beach for vehicles. At the head of these and in other places *wiederstands-nests* (WN or strongpoints) were built: mine-fields, machine-gun nests, anti-tank ditches and linked slit trenches.

On the bluffs, massive walls protected the larger emplacements from seaward bombardment and observation. A system of deep, narrow firing trenches along the crest enabled observers to direct presighted artillery, mortar and incendiary fire with deadly accuracy. Anywhere on the beach Allied troops were easy prey for German machine-guns.

Convinced that a landing would come at high tide, Rommel had extensive minefields laid inland and in the bluffs, with barbed wire entanglements up to the shingle bank.

Staggered rows of stakes, V-shaped wooden ramps and two-metre (6.5ft) high 'Czech Hedgehogs' (welded angular knots of metal designed to rip open the bellies of the landing craft) were scattered 50 to 70 metres (55–77yds) apart seaward of the high tide mark. To most of these, mines were attached. Most formidable of all were the 'Belgian gates', massive iron frame-works placed opposite the draws 200 to 300 metres (220–330yds) below the high tide mark.

On D-Day, 6 June 1944, two natural hazards strengthened the Germans' position. Unusually strong tides concealed treacherous offshore sand bars while metre-deep (3.3ft) runnels scoured parallel to the tidal flats could make the difference between life and death to a wading man with 30kg (66lbs) on his back.

Even though only half of Rommel's planned fortifications and a much smaller fraction of the mine-fields inland were complete, this was the one sector along the Normandy coast that had anything like the kind of cordon defence which the Field Marshal was counting on to stop the Allies on the beaches. Omaha was a terrible prospect for anyone brave enough to attempt a landing there.

BELOW: Defences of this type, designed for the Pas de Calais beaches, aimed to rip the bottoms from landing craft.

Rommel's frequent inspections accelerated the work. The mined wooden ramps at Omaha proved to be more numerous than expected.

WHY LAND AT OMAHA?

'The initial landings must be made on the widest possible front.'

GENERAL SIR BERNARD MONTGOMERY, ARMY COMMANDER

If Omaha held most of the advantages for the enemy, why did the Allied commanders choose to land there? The simple reason is that other options were ruled out: Belgium and the Calais area were heavily defended and within easy reach of German reinforcements; Brittany was too far, and in any case its beaches were unsuitable. The focus inevitably fell on Normandy.

A plan of summer 1943 had advocated a three-division assault supported by two parachute brigades, landing along 48km (30 miles) of beaches (later known as Omaha, Gold, Juno and Sword). In October, Eisenhower (the Supreme Commander) judged the assault to be far too feeble and confused; there was general acclaim among the other commanders for the need of a much stronger assault over a wider front if there was to be a chance of success.

Ike therefore instructed Montgomery to draw up a new plan. Monty's counter-proposal, Operation OVERLORD, involved one American and one British Army, consisting together of eight divisions (five land and three airborne), a landing to include in the American sector the east coast of the Cotentin peninsula, with the aim to secure Cherbourg within seven days and Saint-Lô within nine.

It was logical that the Americans would land at the western end of this stretch, for their

1.5 million troops were stationed mainly in the west of England, Wales and Northern Ireland.

The Allies knew the Omaha terrain was difficult and that the beach was heavily fortified, but once Lower Normandy had been identified as the best option at the Quebec conference of August 1943, there had never been any other choice but to go for it. However, the Allied planners and commanders held several advantages over the enemy.

The British had managed to decrypt the German code machine, Enigma (the Ultra project), while their American colleagues had penetrated the Magic codes of the Japanese. (Unwittingly the Japanese ambassador in Berlin transmitted several pieces of useful intelligence.) By contrast, the Germans had failed to crack Allied codes; even worse for them, all their agents in the UK had been 'turned' and were under British control. The Allies also received a

ABOVE LEFT: Eisenhower and Montgomery disagreed on many issues, but never over the necessity to land at Omaha beach.

CENTRE LEFT: Gen. Omar Bradley, commander of US 1st Army.

LEFT: Rangers Jack Bramkamp ('barber') and Elmer Olander ('client'), both died on the cliff assault at Pointe de la Percée (above right).

Charlie sector: steep bluffs merge into the sheer 30-metre (100ft) cliffs of the Pointe de la Percée. The Rangers and the 116th battled all day to secure this western flank. Lt. Charles Parker of the 5th Rangers with 23 men managed to advance through enemy lines 8km (5 miles) west from Dog Red to reach the Pointe du Hoc from the landward side at 2100 hours: a D-Day record.

ABOVE: Rangers training near Weymouth. Many US units landed at Omaha in British-crewed Royal Navy landing craft.

defences, while Allied aerial dominance prevented the Luftwaffe from monitoring the intense pre-invasion activity of the Allies. The Germans were only allowed to see the fake army 'assembling' in south-east England.

For OVERLORD to succeed, an exact knowledge of the beaches was vital, and in the months before D-Day the Allies also mounted several reconnaissance missions from midget submarines (X-craft). Operating at night, once across the Channel, special teams swam ashore under the noses of the Germans. On Omaha, they measured beach gradients and took soil and sand samples to check that 34-ton tanks could cross the tidal flats. All went well, although at one point a German guard tripped over a measuring line and cursed . . .

(The British also used X-craft on D-Day to guide in the landing craft. The Americans, worried that this could compromise security, did not. As a result, in the first wave onto Omaha, only one company would come in at the right spot.)

constant stream of valuable information from the French Resistance. They monitored troop movements and drew plans of gun batteries in the areas behind the invasion beaches. Those conscripted to plant beach obstacles paced out the distances between them as they worked.

High-speed American P38 Lightnings came back daily with photographs of German

AN INCOMPLETE PICTURE

'It should not be surprising if we discovered that the 352nd Division has one regiment up and two to play.'

Brigadier Williams, Montgomery's intelligence officer

In looking for reasons why the action at Omaha beach proved so costly in lives, it would seem that despite the advantages mentioned the Allies' intelligence jigsaw was far from complete.

Resistance reports from France were sent either by radio or by pigeon. However, in the two months before D-Day, many birds were shot en route and vital intelligence lost. Moreover, not all the information that got through was heeded. For example, on 16 April 1944, the Resistance reported that Allied bombing had damaged one gun on the Pointe du Hoc and caused five others to be withdrawn beyond the coast road, 960 metres (1,000 yards) inland. Yet the D-Day fireplan, and the plan that the Rangers would take out the guns supposed to be on the clifftop, remained unchanged.

For fear of guns aimed at the fleet, US forces disembarked in open seas, out of range and in the dark. But out of over 1,200 warships and a similar number of merchantmen involved in Operation NEPTUNE, only one destroyer was sunk by coastal batteries. At the same time, German gun emplacements designed to rake the beach with enfilading fire (from end to end), went undetected.

LEFT: Ernest Barker of Easland, Texas, and his guitar, leaving southern England on 9 June.

FAR LEFT: Troops in training disembark into Higgins boats. On D-Day 10 of 200 craft would be lost in the process.

In some cases it was simply a failure in intelligence gathering. The Allies knew only of the 800 Germans of the 716th Division in the Omaha area. Neither agents nor the Resistance detected the silent redeployment of over 12,000 men of the 352nd Division, an outfit of battle-hardened older officers from the eastern front, commanding highly-trained and deadly keen young recruits in a state of full combat readiness.

The division was still thought to be at Saint-Lô, 45km (28 miles) from Omaha, unable to be brought into action until 17 hours after H-hour, the time of landing. But on 4 June Brigadier Williams, Monty's intelligence officer, delivered the warning quoted above. Perhaps the British

Medics and litter-bearers board their LCTs (Landing Craft Tanks). Within three weeks the US medical force alone in France came to over 30,000.

LEFT: 'Over-paid, over-sexed and over here' was how the British characterized the 1.5 million Americans waiting to cross into France from the UK.

turn of phrase was lost on the Americans. Suffice to say, General Bradley only learned the truth about the 352nd Division after the landing craft had been sealed. It was too late.

Moreover the 352nd had two regiments 'up', not one as Williams had feared. Detected neither by Ultra nor the Resistance, an extra regiment had been assigned to the 352nd. The division was more than ready to give a good account of itself, as the grim events of D-Day were to prove.

RIGHT: At Omaha, front-line GIs were shocked to find the enemy so well-prepared, so well-concealed and their positions so undamaged.

THUNDER IN THE SKY

'Where', I yelled to no one in particular,
'is the damned Air Corps?'
ROBERT WALKER, CAPTAIN, 29TH DIVISION, 0625 HOURS 6 JUNE

For American forces assigned to Omaha, the D-Day story began at 0251 hours on Tuesday 6 June 1944, when the amphibious command ship USS *Ancon* dropped anchor 18km (11 miles) from the coast of occupied Europe. Overhead 1,300 RAF heavy bombers roared out to drop around 5,000 tons of bombs between the Seine and Cherbourg under cover of darkness. Before daybreak nearly 500 B17s set out on a mission to crater Omaha beach from 6,600 metres (20,000 feet) and knock out the German strong-points. But the cloud cover was total. For fear of hitting Allied troops, the planes delayed bomb release for 30 seconds. No bombs fell on the beach or bluffs; most dropped up to 3km (1.5 miles) or more inland. Over 100 planes flew back to the UK fully loaded. Critically for the landing forces, the 'milk-run' had failed. However, in the final moments prior to H-Hour, 18 medium bombers of the 9th Air Force came in at low altitude to saturate the emplacements of the Pointe du Hoc. This was to make a significant difference there.

Meanwhile out at sea, Task Force 124 included the 32,000-ton battleship USS *Texas* and the heavy cruiser USS *Arkansas*, two Royal Navy light cruisers, two Free French cruisers and 11 destroyers. At first light, the shore batteries at Longues and Port-en-Bessin opened up at the fleet. This met with an immediate response from the sea, and in 20 minutes Longues fell silent. Ernest Hemingway, the writer likened the noise of shells from the USS *Texas* to that of whole railway trains being thrown across the sky. Six hundred shells, each weighing nearly a ton, fell on the Pointe du Hoc and into the cliffs. The ship's secondary guns fired on Vierville. But no response ever came from the much-feared guns at the Pointe du Hoc, 5km (3 miles) to the east.

The naval bombardment of Omaha came to a shrieking climax in the last 10 minutes prior to landing with the launch from landing craft of 10,000 rockets. But Spitfire pilots flying up and down through the black smoke looking for the fall of shells reported that many either crashed into the sea ahead of the troops, or overshot the bluffs.

Disembarkation of infantry and engineers from ships into landing craft began 18km (11 miles) offshore at 0300 hours, in heaving, open seas that hampered their journey and brought back their breakfast. Men were packed like sardines in an open can, their feet awash in bilge water mingled with their own and their neighbours' vomit. Worse still for the operation, an 18-knot wind coupled with a strong current was driving them inexorably east, away from their objectives and towards the obstacles which Rommel had prepared for them.

ABOVE: Awaiting H-Hour: a still recreating this from the film *Saving Private Ryan*.

ABOVE: 22 May: Douglas A20 'Havoc' bombers attack the Pointe du Hoc. The five surviving guns of the 15 April attack had been moved 960 metres (1,000yds) inland.

LEFT: With 79 Shermans knocked out on the beach, after 0930 hours Allied warships proved vital in shifting the balance of firepower in the Americans' favour.

LEFT: Only 9 different pictures survived out of the 72 taken in the water on D-Day by famous war photographer Robert Capa: here men of the 16th Regiment crouch behind mined ramps which the engineers had orders to destroy.

Behind them in the darkness things were going equally badly. Ten landing craft sank alongside their ships; most of the tankdozers and all 26 pieces of heavy artillery slid off the top-heavy amphibious trucks (DUKWS) and into the sea. The 32 amphibious Duplex Drive tanks (see panel), were disembarked, only for 27 of them to sink like stones, taking some of their crew with them. Most of the convention-ally waterproofed tanks on board landing craft, and able to fire on the approach, did reach the shore. Although unable to get off the beach they provided vital support, the fall of their shells being used to guide in naval salvoes.

The 34-ton M4 Sherman was the standard Allied World War II tank. To give immediate fire support to the landing, 32 of these were adapted as Duplex Drive amphibious vehicles. Each had two propellers and a collapsible rubberized canvas folding screen raised by compressed air from a bottle attached to the front armour.

As the tank hit the shore the screen collapsed, leaving the turret a clear field of fire. At Omaha, only five made it to the shore. At Utah all but four landed safely – but weren't needed.

'I watched the movie *The Longest Day* and they came charging off those boats and across the beach like banshees, but that isn't the way it happened. You came off the craft, hit the water, and if you didn't get down in it you were going to get shot .... The water was turning red from the blood. There were dead men floating in the water and live men acting dead, letting the tide take them in ....'
Sgt. John Slaughter, 116th Infantry Regiment, aged 19

ABOVE: 91 men were killed and 64 wounded of 170 men in the first wave onto Dog Green.

'I tried to get my men off the boat and make it somehow to get under the seawall. We waded to the sand and threw ourselves down and the men were frozen, unable to move. My radioman had his head blown off three yards from me. The beach was covered with bodies, men with no legs, no arms – God, it was awful.' Sgt. Harry Bare, 116th Regiment

ALL THE WAY IN

'As our boat touched sand and the ramp went down I became a visitor to hell.'
HARRY PARLEY, 116TH INFANTRY REGIMENT

After only 45 minutes' firing the naval guns ceased abruptly at 0630 hours to allow the landings to begin, but things went badly wrong. Some landing craft grounded on the hidden sandbars 1.5km (a mile) out; others had their bottoms ripped out by the lurking obstacles. Six craft containing men of Company A were on target facing the Vierville draw, but found themselves with no supporting engineers, artillery or tanks; a dozen other craft were swept eastward by wind and current, 3km (two miles) out of position.

To their dismay, troops approaching the beach could see that gun emplacements in the bluffs remained largely undamaged. But having spent three or more hours in stinking anti-gas clothing, ashen with seasickness and fear, and weighed down by 30kg (66lbs) of equipment, they were craving to get down the ramp. As the film *Saving Private Ryan* so graphically illustrated, the troops in the first wave – experienced men of the 1st Infantry Division and young, untried National Guardsmen of the 116th Regiment, 29th Division – disembarked onto a grotesque killing-ground. Instead of landing as nine companies evenly spaced along the beach, they found themselves drawn to the very worst concentrations of German firepower and passive defence.

Moreover, the 116th had counted on the artillery of the amphibious tanks to take up the task. Most of these were now sunk.

In the minutes following, Company A sustained 96 per cent casualties without firing a shot; over 800 men of 2,000 in the 116th Regiment would be killed or wounded by the day's end.

A third of the men landing at Omaha that day were engineers whose mission was to blow 16 corridors through Rommel's beach obstacles before the tide covered them. By the end of the morning over 40 per cent of them were casualties, their task made virtually impossible by the intense fire and tidal waters deepening by a metre (3.3 feet) an hour. America's Gettysburg of the Second World War had begun.

ABOVE: A more orderly scene as men of the 2nd Division land on 7 June. Amphibious trucks (DUKWs or ducks) and half-tracks are ashore.

ASSAULT ON THE POINTE DU HOC

'Anybody would be a fool to try this. It was crazy then, and it's crazy now.'

LIEUTENANT COLONEL JAMES RUDDER, CO, 2ND RANGER BATTALION IN 1954

'Lead the Way Rangers' is their proud motto and now the search words for their website: a still from *The Longest Day*.

The guns on the promontory at the Pointe du Hoc threatened both American beaches. The six 155mm pivoting howitzers represented the greatest concentration of German firepower anywhere along the Normandy coast. It was the Rangers' job to take them out.

The US Army Rangers had been founded in 1942 and had been partly instructed by the British commandos on whom they were modelled. For many months the men of the 2nd and 5th Ranger Battalions had been trained specifically for Pointe du Hoc. It would be their first combat mission.

On the landward side minefields, defences and 20mm guns made the battery a veritable fortress. On the seaward side, sheer cliffs the height of a nine-storey apartment block were thought to be protection enough.

The plan was that at 0630 hours Companies D, E and F, under the command of Lt. Col. Rudder, would lead the main assault on both flanks of the Pointe du Hoc. At the same time, Company C was to attack the Pointe de la Percée 4km (2.5 miles) to the east. Companies A and B were to wait for a signal at 0700 hours either to reinforce the action at the Pointe du Hoc or to land with the 5th Ranger Battalion at Dog Green 6km (4 miles) to the east. From there, they and the 116th Regiment of the 29th Division were to cross the bocage to reinforce Rudder from the landward side.

Company C landed first at 0645 hours. Almost immediately, out of 68 men 19 were killed and 18 wounded as they struggled to reach the cliffs. At this point they were alone, the nearest surviving Americans being 3km (2 miles) to the east on Dog Red, or a whole world away on Utah beach to the west.

While the foot of the cliffs provided the survivors with some shelter, it was no place to linger, as grenades and mortars were continually exploding at their feet.

This was where their months of assault training came in, and by 0730 hours the best climbers were on top, having used bayonets as handholds. They then lowered ropes from minefield stakes for the others to monkey-walk up the cliffs. The battle to make the westernmost draw safe would continue all day.

Rough seas, seasickness, poor navigation and German fire caused Companies D, E and F to come in too far east. Correcting the mistake cost time, lives and three landing craft. At 0710 hours the remaining ten craft hit the churning foreshore of the Pointe du Hoc together.

Many things went against them. Rocket-fired grappling irons fell short, weighed down by sodden ropes; because of craters on the beach the DUKWs could not deploy their ladders. So with sectional ladders, bayonets,

ABOVE: The Pointe du Hoc today, capped by the Ranger Memorial (1954).

grenades, wet, muddy ropes and bare hands the Rangers began a perilous climb up the cliff face, part of it a huge slippery scree of broken limestone caused by the naval bombardment.

The garrison above normally consisted of some 200 men, but the low-level bomber sweep and intense naval gunfire had pushed many of them back, saving many Rangers' lives. By 0730 hours, 180 Rangers had reached the top, a burning lunar landscape where thousands of tons of high explosive had fallen. They met only slight resistance. Rudder's casualties were still relatively light, another testament to their superb training and courage. The craters provided useful cover, tragically missing elsewhere on Omaha, as they headed for the gun emplacements and observation posts on the edge of the promontory.

FAR LEFT: German troops in one of the many strongpoints that defended Omaha.

LEFT: Rangers diverted from the Pointe du Hoc came in with National Guard troops on Dog.

RIGHT: Rangers on the cliff on 8 June. Three methods of scaling the cliff are in evidence.

THE MYSTERY OF THE MISSING GUNS

'The most dangerous mission of D-Day.'

LIEUTENANT GENERAL OMAR N. BRADLEY, COMMANDER, 1ST US ARMY

For many months, Lt. Col. Rudder's men had undergone gruelling and realistic training specifically for the Pointe du Hoc. Yet when they reached what they thought were the guns, they found only telephone poles in disguise. Two new emplacements had clearly never housed the guns they were meant for; indeed the Resistance had reported 50 days earlier that the mobile artillery had been moved back. Yet this possibility had not been communicated to the men, nor had it in any way changed the air and naval bombardment plan.

A platoon of 22 men, under Sgt. Leonard Lomell, was sent ahead to cover the coastal road. They swept over the headland in the teeth of enemy fire from the maze of tunnels and bunkers. Ten of them died. Plunging down a double hedgerow off the coastal road, Lomell and his friend, Sgt. Jack Kuhn, came upon the guns in an apple orchard. Beside them lay neat stacks of unprotected ammunition. To their further surprise, only 70–90 metres (75–100 yards) away in a neighbouring field were about 75 German soldiers being addressed

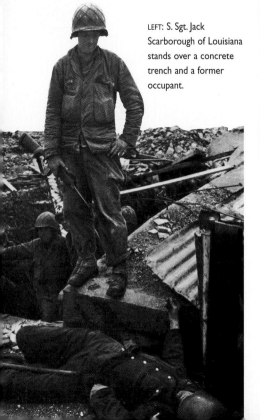

LEFT: S. Sgt. Jack Scarborough of Louisiana stands over a concrete trench and a former occupant.

by an officer. They were keeping their distance until ordered to fire – orders which would never come. Covered by Kuhn, Lomell destroyed two guns with silent, smokeless grenades which melted the recoil mechanism. Lomell then ran back to get more grenades, yet when he returned the Germans were still unaware of what had happened to their guns. By 0830 hours the remaining three had been disabled in the same way.

An instant later there was a tremendous explosion that sent showers of debris onto them: the ammunition dump had been blown up, creating the vast crater which can still be seen today. Following orders, the Rangers then took up position straddling the coastal road to await reinforcements. But with the main force blocked on the beach over the next few hours only a few stragglers were to arrive.

During the next 48 hours the Germans of the 352nd Division mounted three counter-attacks. By the time relief arrived on 8 June, only 50 men were still able to fight: of the 225 Rangers in the 2nd Battalion, 81 were killed, and most of the others wounded; all were exhausted. This was the human price paid to ensure the guns, which had been missed by air and navy firepower, were neutralised at the critical time.

The original fireplan – with Pointe du Hoc the priority target - and strategy of attack had not been changed in the light of the resistance report sent on 16 April, which may not have reached the right authority or not been believed. However the acting operational commander, Captain Lytle, on his transport at Weymouth on 5 June, and inebriated, began shouting that the guns were no longer on the Pointe du Hoc, and lashed out at the medic trying to restrain him. He was hastily hospitalized.

Rudder, although General Huebner had forbidden it, insisted on leading the operation personally. By destroying the guns, drawing the German 914th Regiment from the beach, and dominating the left flank of the operation, the colonel and his Rangers critically influenced the outcome at Omaha.

THE TURNING OF THE TIDE

'There are two kinds of people are going to stay on this beach, the dead and those who are going to die. Now let's get the hell out of here!'

COLONEL GEORGE TAYLOR

The first German resistance point was captured at 0900 hours by which time some 600 men had reached the bluffs. But for most of the morning there was little forward movement; the rising water drowned the wounded and restricted the beach to nothing. Vehicles were blocked by the shingle bank or the sea wall, and withering fire continued to bear down on the hapless troops. Corridors through the obstacles were few and Higgins boats began piling into three cleared lanes making them easy targets for German gunners. Ordered to hold off, they were reported to be 'milling round offshore like a stampeded herd of cattle'.

Yet an hour later the first reports of German surrender began to filter in, much to the relief of the generals, who had been plunged into gloom by the morning's reports. The defenders were running out of ammunition, while Allied ships were piling in. With the assault plan in tatters it became a matter of individual initiative. The surviving US infantry, despite being shell-shocked and without radios, officers or artillery, were beginning to move up the bluffs between the draws and wheedle out the hitherto invisible enemy.

There were many outstanding examples of successful exhortation and command for otherwise leaderless and disorientated young men, such as the one quoted above. Some have been enshrined in the mottoes of the units involved.

The navies were to be crucial in unblocking the situation for the infantry. As no messages came from the fire-parties on shore, ships had to rely on what they could see for themselves. At 0930 hours eleven destroyers were brought in to home in on targets of opportunity. They came steaming parallel to the coast, firing continuously, at times scraping their bottoms on the seabed. One of the German emplacements was actually seen to fall off the cliff and onto the beach, another to blow up. USS *McCook* fired nearly 1,000 rounds on D-Day.

In subsequent days, USS *Texas* was firing at targets up to 13kms (8 miles) inland, deliberately heeling itself over to get extra range.

ABOVE: Each beached LST was capable of disgorging 20 tanks or 120 small vehicles.

LEFT: No authorized photographs show the full horror of Omaha beach on D-Day.

LEFT: Colleville church. Local towers were 'lopped off' by naval guns to prevent their use as observation posts.

BELOW INSET: Plasma is given to a wounded man of the 5th Special Engineer Brigade on Fox Green.

By noon infantry, having gone over the bluffs, had occupied Vierville. The tide began to drop back. At 1330 hours a general advance up the slopes began. Although the draws were still in German hands, the nut had been cracked.

From 1430 hours Force B, the second wave, was able to land, the men looking on in awed silence at the terrible evidence of the morning's carnage. By 1530 hours the divisional staffs were ashore. By 1730 hours the engineers were preparing the beaches for unloading on a massive scale. By nightfall 34,250 men and nearly 3,000 vehicles were ashore, in a bridgehead no more than a kilometre (1,100 yards) deep. It would take six days to link up with US forces at Utah; six weeks to reach Saint-Lô. By 16 June, over a quarter of a million men and 35,000 vehicles had landed on Omaha beach alone: an entire prefabricated port, Mulberry 'A', was taking shape. By mid-July the Americans were landing 35,000 tons of material each day. In less than a year, the story which began on D-Day would end with Allied forces in Belsen and Berlin.

From 8 June the beach was no longer under enemy fire and men and material could come ashore in safety.

17

WE SHALL REMEMBER THEM

'This embattled shore, portal of freedom, is forever hallowed by the ideals, the valor and the sacrifices of our fellow countrymen.'

The Normandy National American Cemetery at Colleville-Saint-Laurent is the only American cemetery built on the site of a battlefield. Here, overlooking the Easy Red sector, 9,387 war graves aligned in rows make a deeply impressive sight. Over one thousand of these bear the date 6 June 1944. Some 14,000 bodies, over 60 per cent of the total, were repatriated to the US in the late 1940s.

Losses on land and sea off Omaha on D-Day totalled over 2,000 – more than all the other beaches put together. The little US town of Bedford, Virginia (population 2,000) lost 23 of its 46 sons in Company A. Eleven of them lie here.

The cemetery was inaugurated in July 1956 on land that has the status of American soil, a gift, free of tax, in perpetuity from the French people. The cliffs and fields around have been purchased by the French state to protect the site's tranquillity.

The gravestones are in Lasa marble from Italy. Most are simple Latin crosses; there are 147 Stars of David and 307 graves contain unidentified soldiers, 'known but to God'. Of the 38 pairs of brothers buried in the cemetery the most famous are Theodore and Quentin Roosevelt, sons of President Teddy Roosevelt (D28: 45 and 46). Quentin's is a First World War grave.

Also there are Preston and Robert Niland (F15: 11 and 12) whose story inspired *Saving Private Ryan*. Uniquely in an overseas cemetery, a father and son also lie together: Col. Ollie Reed and Ollie Reed Jnr. (E20: 19 and 20). Three graves inscribed in gold indicate winners of the Medal of Honor (the American equivalent of the VC): Brig. Gen. Theodore Roosevelt, commander on Utah beach; Technical Sgt. Frank Peregory of the 116th Infantry Regiment (G21: 7), who has his own memorial outside Grandcamp, and 1st Lt. Jimmie Monteith Jnr. of the 16th Infantry Regiment (I20: 12) who led and organized repeated attacks off the beach, including twice driving tanks through a minefield. Lt. Turner Turnbull, a native American (E21: 21), led a furious blocking action west of Sainte-Mère-Eglise. Lt. Gen.

ABOVE: America's first cemetery, on Dog White, is inaugurated by an army chaplain.

Lesley McNair, the first 3-star general to be killed, (F28: 42) had led the drive for hard and realistic training of the 'Citizen Army' under General Marshall, and had insisted on seeing combat at first hand, only to be killed by 'friendly fire' outside Saint-Lô.

Here lie the graves of four women, three of whom were black: Red Cross nurses and WACs killed by accidental fire after the war.

The bronze statue of American youth, flanked by battle maps and framed by a semicircular colonnade, reminds us that many of those who died on Omaha beach did so only a short time after graduating from high school. In the rose garden behind is a wall inscribed with the names of 1,557 missing. Of these, 168 are from D-Day, while 489 are from America's second worst naval disaster of the war, the torpedoing and sinking of the troopship USS *Leopoldville* off Cherbourg on 24 December 1944. There was no official release of information nor any enquiry. It is a chilling reminder of the risks involved in mounting the D-Day invasion. Indeed the Allied generals sent thousands of their finest young men into action, knowing that their planners anticipated 25 per cent overall casualties among the initial assault regiments, far higher than was actually sustained – except at Omaha.

SECOND INFANTRY DIVISION
UNITED STATES OF AMERICA
FOR THOSE WHO FOUGHT AND DIED FOR FREEDOM
1944-45

ABOVE: The grave of Brig. Gen. Theodore Roosevelt.

LEFT: Each division has its memorial: this is to the 2nd Division at Le Ruquet, Easy Red.